D0205383

Alpine
Flowers

SIGHTING AND ENJOYING

KOMPASS
Nature Guide

The author **Dr. Christine Jaitner,** born 1952, studied zoology a
systematic botany at Innsbruck University. She received h
Ph. D. in the field of protozoology.

Impressum
74 color photos
 2 color plates
 2 illustrations

Text: Dr. Christine Jaitner, Patsch
English Translation: Mary Heaney Margreiter, Innsbruck
Cover Design: Günther Haas, Innsbruck
Color Plates and Illustrations: Heinz Schwanninger, Absam
Management and Editing: Reinhard Strohmeier, KOMPASS, Innsbruck

Color Photos:
Front Cover: Rhaetian Poppy (Fiebrandt)
Back Cover: Hauser Kaibling Mountain (Haas)
Insert: Christmas Rose (Geiersperger)

Baier: p. 65. Bernardinatti: p. 56, 66. Bildagentur Fiebrandt: p. 8, 11, 13,
15, 16, 17, 20, 21, 23, 24, 26, 28, 31, 32, 33, 34, 38, 44, 47, 52, 53, 58, 59,
68, 74, 76, 77. Brüssler: p. 9, 12, 36, 54, 67, 73. Geiersperger/Bildagentur
Wagner: p. 10, 29, 40, 46, 60, 64, 69. Geissler: p. 25, 48, 49, 55, 61. Haas
19, 22. Hage: p. 35, 42. Limbrunner: p. 18, 27, 30, 37, 39, 41, 43, 45, 50, 51,
57, 62, 70, 71, 72, 75.

© **Fleischmann & Mair GmbH, Innsbruck/Rum 1991**
Phototype: Raggl Supertype GmbH & Co. KG, Innsbruck
Reproductions: Tiroler Repro, Innsbruck
Printed by: Printers S. r. l., Trient

Publisher's No. 1300
ISBN 3-87051-592-9

ear Nature Friend,

eryone who likes being outdoors and appreciates flora d fauna will enjoy identifying the different plants and imals. This book was conceived to not overburden the ture-watcher in his identification and is intentionally ncise and easy to read.

this KOMPASS Nature Guide you will find 70 of the most mmon and abundant Alpine plants. It should be mention-that these plants also occur in other mountainous re-ns of Europe. Since a solely textual description of the in-idual plants is not sufficient to guarantee proper identifi-tion, the color photos were so chosen to show the plants 'heir true colors and natural surroundings. The plants are marily ordered according to the color of their flowers. thin this color group, they are systematically classified.

e names are given both in English (for example Least mrose) and according to the „binary nomenclature" de-ed by Linné, namely the genus (primula) and species inima). Several genera (or genuses) form a family ceae) and several families an order (-ales). The orders ke up the classes (-atae). These are grouped in sec-ns and the kingdom.

nce each plant is known under a variety of names in glish, this guide uses the most common name. This is owed by the plant's scientific name, the family to which it ongs, characters, habitat, distribution and special re-rks.

e listings "Date Seen" and "Place" will give you the ance to note your observations on the spot.

joy the flora of the Alps!

Dr. Christine Ja...

3

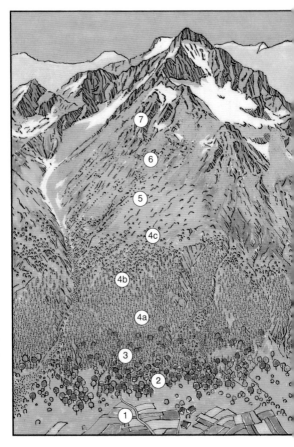

1 **Planar Belt:** grain fields
2 **Colline Belt:** deciduous forests, meadows
3 **Mountain Belt:** mixed forests
4a **Lower Subalpine Belt:** coniferous forests to tree line
4b **Mid-Subalpine Belt:** knee-timber belt
4c **Upper Subalpine Belt:** dwarf-shrub belt with berries
5 **Alpine Belt:** Alpine grasslands
6 **Subnival Belt:** pioneer grasslands belt
7 **Nival Belt:** cushion grasslands belt with mosses and lichen

4

Altitude Belts of the Alps

Altitude and dropping temperatures determine the following **altitude belts** or vegetation belts:

Planar Belt: grain fields, residual forests

Colline Belt: oak and hornbeam woods, meadows, vines

Mountain Belt: 800—1000 m, red beeches, spruce, larches

Subalpine Belt: 1600—2000 m
- Lower Subalpine Belt:
  last coniferous forests (spruce, larches, arolla pines) before tree line
- Mid-Subalpine Belt:
  knee pines
  Upper Subalpine Belt:
  dwarf-shrub belt with crowberry, magnolia vine, cranberry

Alpine Belt: approx. 1300 m, belt of Alpine grasslands, pastures

Subnival Belt: approx. 2600—2800 m, pioneer grasslands belt

Nival Belt: cushion plant belt and cryptogamic belt (mosses, lichen, algae)

Vegetation Forms in the Various Habitats

Rock crevices:	temperature-insensitive, resistant to snow and sand storms, insensitive to dryness, cushion plants, rosettes, dwarf subshrubs
Screes:	debris creeper, debris wanderer with taproot, debris coverer with rooting branches, debris holder with firm grasp
Snowbeds:	extremely short vegetation period, green parts and flowers often spend winter under the snow, dwarf growth, dwarf willows, least willows
Springs:	moss, saxifrages, butterworts, marsh marigold, birdseye primrose, cotton sedge

High-Alpine Grasslands:	many plants with evaporatic protection such as hai leaves, mountain avens, sax frages, moss campion, ede weiss, trumpet gentian
Mats:	cultivated meadows, crocu grasses, dandelion
Tall Herb Communities:	common monkshood, thistl helleborine
Overfertilized Alms:	over-fertilized soils on alpir pastures, docks
White Bent Grasslands:	result of overgrazing, whi bent
Dwarf Shrub Heath:	woody plants, cranberry, bea berry, alpenrose
Knee-Timber Thicket:	garland flower, alpine clema tis, mountain pine, green ald

Plant Parts

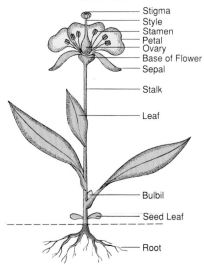

- Stigma
- Style
- Stamen
- Petal
- Ovary
- Base of Flower
- Sepal
- Stalk
- Leaf
- Bulbil
- Seed Leaf
- Root

efinitions

ompletely protected: These plants must not be picked, amaged or destroyed. In their fresh state they may not be ansplanted, purchased, transported or sold. This protecn covers all parts of the plant.

otected: These plants are completely or partially protect-d, depending on the country where they are found.

artially protected: The protection is limited to certain pends, development forms, locations and parts and exudes commercial trade or collecting.

ndemic: plant only occurs within a certain region

hizome: underground, horizontal root

onoecious: male and female flowers on the same plant

ioecious: male and female plants

isexual: one flower has male and female plant parts

: male
: female

luster of Rush Flowers: Flowers of the rushes and edges; lower branches of the flowers protrude above the pper ones.

poisonous
protected

lower Colors:

white	
yellow	
red	
violet	
blue	
green	

Alpine Buttercup

Ranunculus alpestris   Buttercup Family;

Characters: perennial, five white petals, solitary flower; petals and sepals fall off soon, leaves 3—5-lobed; lobe; palmately lobed, stems hairless, height 5—15 cm. **Flower:** June—Sept. **Habitat:** calcareous Alps, rocky debris 1500—2800 m. **Special Remarks:** Poisonous!

Date Seen:

Place:

Glacier Crowfoot

Ranunculus glacialis   Buttercup Family; † ⚠

Characters: perennial rosette, bisexual, five white necta-
ries often tinged with purple, umbrella-like cluster, 5 green
sepals; stem prostrate to upright, thick, leaves alternate,
composite, height 5—15 cm. **Flowers:** July—Aug. **Habitat:**
rocky debris, rock, 2300—4200 m. **Distribution:** Alps, Pyrenees, Iceland. **Special Remarks:** Poisonous! Protected!
Medicinal herb.

Date Seen:

Place:

Christmas Rose

Helleborus niger Buttercup Family; † ⚠

Characters: perennial, solitary white flowers, 1—3 scal
bracts on stem; overwintering leaves, 7—6-parted, blac
rootstock, height 15—30 cm. **Flowers:** Dec.—Apr. **Habitat**
woods, 0—1800 m. **Distribution:** calcareous Alps, Apen
nines, Balkans. **Special Remarks:** Poisonous! Protected
Seeks out limestone.

Date Seen:

Place:

Narcissus-Flowered Anemone

Anemona narcissiflora   Buttercup Family; † ⚠

Characters: perennial, white, often pink-flushed below, umbels of 3—8 flowers in a many-lobed bract, 5—6 petals; leaves palmately parted, stem and leaf underside hairy, height 30—60 cm. **Flowers:** May—July. **Habitat:** woods, rush, 1500—2500 m. **Distribution:** calcareous Alps. **Special Remarks:** Protected! Poisonous!

Date Seen:

Place:

Alpine Moon Daisy

Leucanthemopsis alpina   Daisy Fam.

Characters: perennial cushion plant, bisexual, flower heads with white rays, yellow tubular florets; leaves opposit 1-pinnate, rhizome, height 5—15 cm. **Flowers:** July—Au **Habitat:** short grass, rocky places 1600—3900 m. **Distribu tion:** Alps, Pyrenees, Carpathians.

Date Seen:

Place:

Mountain Avens

Dryas octopetala   Rose Family

Characters: perennial dwarf-shrub, bisexual, solitary flowers with 8 petals, achene with shaggy white papus (flight organ), flowers white; leaves elliptical, evergreen, scalloped, white–woolly beneath, taproot, height 3–10 cm. **Flowers:** May–Aug. **Habitat:** screes, rock, 1100–2500 m. **Distribution:** Northern Europe, Alps, on limestone, dolomite, common.

Date Seen:

Place:

Blue Saxifrage

Saxifraga caesia   Saxifrage Famil

Characters: perennial cushion plant, white, 5 petals, 1—
flowers per stalk with sticky glandular secretion; leave
in rosettes, small, 5—9 limestone pores or entirely lim
encrusted, thick leaves, height 5—10 cm. **Flower:**
July—Sept. **Habitat:** rock crevices, screes, 500—2500 n
pioneer plant. **Distribution:** calcareous Alps.

Date Seen:

Place:

Mossy Saxifrage

Saxifraga bryoides   Saxifrage Family; ⚠

Characters: perennial flat cushion plant, white, center yellow, 5 petals, stalk with 1—3 flowers; glandular hairs on
stalk, leaves rigid, oblong lance-shaped, unnotched,
height 1—5 cm. **Flowers:** June—Aug. **Habitat:** rocky and
stony places, to 2400 m. **Distribution:** only Central Alps.
Special Remarks: Protected!

Date Seen:

Place:

Alpine Mouse Ear

Cerastium alpinum   Pink Fami

Characters: perennial creeper, white, 5 petals cleft, 1–
flowers at base of leaves; leaves oval, entire plant hai
height 5—20 cm. **Flowers:** July—Sept. **Habitat:** rocky pl
ces, 1800—2800 m. **Distribution:** Alps, Northern Europ

Date Seen:

Place:

Swiss Rock Jasmine

Androsace helvetica   Primrose Family; ⚠

Characters: perennial cushion plant, cushion very dense, white petals with yellow eye, stemless flowers; leaves oval, entire plant hairy, grayish, height 1–12 cm. **Flowers:** May–July. **Habitat:** rocks, 1500–3500 m. **Distribution:** western calcareous Alps. **Special Remarks:** Protected!

Date Seen:

Place:

Alpine Butterwort

Pinguicula alpina Butterwort Family; ⌐

Characters: perennial, erect rosette, bisexual, solita⌐
flower spurred, yellow spots in throat, white; leaves oblon⌐
margins inrolled, basal rosette, rhizome, height 5—15 cr⌐
Flowers: May—June. **Habitat:** bogs, wet grasslands, ⌐
limestone, 800—2000 m. **Distribution:** Alps, Alpine foothill⌐
rare. **Special Remarks:** insectivorous, protected!

Date Seen:

Place:

Edelweiss

eontopodium alpinum   Daisy Family; ⚠

haracters: perennial rosette, bisexual, flowers packed in
ompound heads surrounded by woolly-white bracts, only
sc of tubular florets, white; leaves lance-shaped, woolly,
ternate, height 5—20 cm. **Flowers:** July—Aug. **Habitat:**
asslands, dry grasslands, pastures, rock, 1700—3500 m.
istribution: Alps, Pyrenees. **Special Remarks:** Entirely
otected! Medicinal herb.

ate Seen:

lace:

Stemless Carline Thistle

Carlina acaulis   Daisy Family; /

Characters: perennial rosette, bisexual, disc of brownis
tubular florets, outer bracts resemble rays, silvery whit
leaves in rosette, pinnately cut, spiny, taproot, height 5
30 cm. **Flowers:** July—Sept. **Habitat:** meadows, fores
grasslands, 700—2900 m. **Distribution:** Europe, commo
Special Remarks: Protected!

Date Seen:

Place:

Scheuchzer's Cotton Sedge

Eriophorum scheuchzeri   Sedge Family

Characters: monocotyledonous, loose, with runners, bi-sexual, spikes with hairy white tuft; stalk cylindrical, upper-most leaf sheathes stalk, short and wide leaf surface, height 15—30 cm. **Flowers:** July—Aug. **Habitat:** ponds, wa-terways, 1500—2600 m. **Distribution:** Alps.

Date Seen:

Place:

Globeflower

Trollis europaeus　　　　　　Buttercup Family; † △

Characters: perennial, erect, bisexual plant, 10 petals 5—10 sepals, spherical when closed, yellow; leaves palmately cut, alternate, rhizome, height 10—55 cm. **Flowers** May—Aug. **Habitat:** damp meadows, bogs, tall herb communities, 900—2500 m. **Distribution:** Europe. **Special Remarks:** Poisonous! Partially protected! Seeks out nitrogen.

Date Seen:

Place:

Wolfsbane

Aconitum vulparia   Buttercup Family; † ⚠

Characters: perennial, erect plant, bisexual, yellow, helmet-like flowers in raceme, leaves alternate, palmately cut, lower leaves long-stemmed, taproot, height 50—110 cm. **Flowers:** June—Aug. **Habitat:** damp forests, grasslands, 500—2500 m. **Distribution:** Alps, Apennines, not common. **Special Remarks:** Highly poisonous! Protected!

Date Seen:

Place:

Rhaetian Poppy

Papaver alpinum ssp. rhaeticum   Poppy Family; ⚠

Characters: perennial with solitary yellow flowers, 4 pe
als, roundish, many stamens; stalk erect, bristly, ur
branched, basal leaves pinnate, plant with milky late>
height 5—15 cm. **Flowers:** July—Aug. **Habitat:** scree
1800—3000 m. **Distribution:** only Western Alps. **Speci**
Remarks: in south-east locations narrow-lobed, reddish
in Northern Alps white! Protected!

Date Seen:

Place:

Alpine Avens

Geum montanum   Rose Family

Characters: perennial, creeping rosette, yellow, 5 petals, mainly solitary flowers, hairy, leaves short-stemmed, pinnate, end leaflet largest, fruit with long, hairy styles, height —40 cm. **Flowers:** May—July. **Habitat:** under-fertilized meadows, pastures, dwarf-shrub heath, frost- and wind-sensitive, 1000—3000 m. **Distribution:** Alps, Central Alps.

Date Seen:

Place:

Auricula

Primula auricula   Primrose Family; ⌐

Characters: perennial rosette, bisexual, flower of joine
petals, yellow, 4—12 flowers per stalk; leaves broad, flesh
grayish-green, mealy, rhizome, height 5—20 cm. **Flower**
Apr.—June. **Habitat:** stony soil, gravel, rock, 800—2600 n
Distribution: Alps, Apennines, Carpathians, rare. **Speci**
Remarks: Endangered! Protected!

Date Seen:

Place:

potted Gentian

entiana punctata   Gentian Family; ⚠

characters: perennial, erect plant, bisexual, flowers bell-shaped, pale yellow with purple spots, whorled, sepal tube th 5 variously long lobes; leaves oval to oblong, tip never und, rhizome, height 20—60 cm. **Flowers:** July—Aug. **abitat:** stony loam, Alpine dwarf-shrub heath, avoids ni-ogen, 1500—2500 m. **Distribution:** Alps, particularly acid cks. **Special Remarks:** Protected! Old medicinal herb.

ate Seen:

ace:

Yellow Genipi

Artemisia mutellina   Daisy Family;

Characters: perennial cushion plant, yellow tubular floret
flowerheads in raceme; leaves finger-shaped, low
leaves twice three-parted, entire plant hairy, heig
10—20 cm. **Flowers:** July—Sept. **Habitat:** rock, scree
mountain crests, 1800—3000 m. **Distribution:** Maritime
Eastern Alps. **Special Remarks:** Protected! Old medicin
herb.

Date Seen:

Place:

rnica

nica montana   Daisy Family; † ⚠

aracters: perennial, erect plant, bisexual, flowerhead of
llow disc florets with yellow rays, ovary with crown of
irs; stem downy, 1—2 pairs of opposite stem leaves, bas-
eaves oval, in rosettes, tough, hairy, aromatic, rhizome,
ight 20—60 cm. **Flowers:** June—Aug. **Habitat:** mead-
s, woods, grasslands, peaty soil, 200—2900 m. **Distri-
tion:** Alps, Apennines, Carpathians. **Special Remarks:**
dangered! Protected! Poisonous! Medicinal herb — de-
nds great caution!

te Seen: **Place:**

Large Flowered Leopardsbane

Doronicum grandiflorum   Daisy Fam

Characters: perennial, erect plant, bisexual, disc of yell
tubular florets with yellow rays; leaves alternate, claspi
stalk, glandular-hairy, rhizome, height 10—50 cm. **Flowe**
July—Aug. **Habitat:** screes, rock crevices, 1700—3200
Distribution: calcareous Alps, Pyrenees, Corsica, r
common.

Date Seen:

Place:

olden Hawksbeard

epis aurea   Daisy Family

aracters: perennial, rosette, orange-yellow rays form
itary flowers, flower bracts and upper stem with dark
en hairs; leaves hairless, lance-shaped, toothed,
ght 20—30 cm. **Flowers:** July—Sept. **Habitat:** mead-
s, pastures, 1000—2500 m. **Distribution:** Alps, northern
kan peninsula.

te Seen:

ce:

Chamois Ragwort

Senecio doronicum   Daisy Fam

Characters: perennial, flowerheads of yellow rays and d
of tubular florets, 1—8 in loose raceme, downy, leaves lo
and narrow, downy, lightly toothed, height 20—50 c
Flowers: July—Aug. **Habitat:** grassy and rocky place
screes, on limestone, 1000—3000 m. **Distribution:** calc
reous Alps.

Date Seen:

Place:

Gray Alpine Groundsel

enecio incanus ssp. carniolicus   Daisy Family

haracters: perennial, yellow flowerheads with 3—6 rays, ·llow tubular florets, heads in umbels; leaves slightly athered (pinnate) or scalloped, gray-green, height 15 cm. **owers:** July—Sept. **Habitat:** grasslands, screes, rock, ·er 2000 m. **Distribution:** east of the Grisons (Graubün- ·n), Allgäu.

ate Seen:

ace:

33

Giant Catsear

Hypochoeris uniflora   Daisy Fam

Characters: perennial rosette, only yellow rays formi
one flowerhead per stem, stem swollen under flowerhea
roughly hairy, sepal with dark hairs; leaves sparsely ha
toothed, height 30—50 cm. **Flowers:** July—Sept. **Habit**
acid soils, mountain forests, seeks out acid so
1000—2500 m. **Distribution:** Central and Southern Alp

Date Seen:

Place:

etuse-Leaved Willow

alix retusa   Willow Family

aracters: dioecious, mat-forming undershrub with root-
branches, few flowers in loose catkins, yellow; leaves
ce as long as wide, tip blunt or notched, hairless, dark
en, later yellow. **Flowers:** June—Oct. **Habitat:** rock,
rees, on limestone, 1500—2500 m. **Distribution:** Alps,
renees, Apennines.

te Seen:

ace:

Mountain Houseleek

Sempervivum montanum   Stonecrop Family;

Characters: perennial rosette with runners, bisexual, da
red to pink, 12—16 petals, flowerheads in umbel; stem a
fleshy stem leaves glandular hairy, basal leaves formi
small dense rosettes, height 5—15 cm. **Flowers:** July—Au
Habitat: stony places, rocks, 1900—3500 m. **Distributic**
Alps, Apennines, Pyrenees. **Special Remarks:** Protecte

Date Seen:

Place:

Purple Saxifrage

axifraga oppositifolia   Saxifrage Family; ⚠

haracters: perennial cushion plant, flowers bloom red,
de to blue, 5 petals, trailing stem covered with 4 conspic-
ous rows of dense leaves; leaves opposite, rigid, height
–5 cm. **Flowers:** Mar.–July. **Habitat:** stony grasslands,
ck, mountain crests, 1700–3500 m. **Distribution:** Alps,
candinavia. **Special Remarks:** Protected!

ate Seen:

lace:

Alpine Rock Jasmine

Androsace alpina   Primrose Family;

Characters: perennial, bisexual cushion plant with taproo
pink to red, also white, solitary flowers with 5 petals; bas
lance-shaped leaves, height 2—6 cm. **Flowers:** July—Au
Habitat: screes, 2000—4200 m. **Distribution:** Alps. **Sp
cial Remarks:** Protected!

Date Seen:

Place:

Moss Campion

Silene acaulis   Pink Family; ⚠

Characters: perennial, cushion plant, bisexual, red solitary flowers with 5 petals, sepals fused; leaves lance-shaped, short, margin ciliated, taproot, height to 5 cm. **Flowers:** June–Aug. **Habitat:** grasslands, rock, screes, 1900–3200 m. **Distribution:** Alps, Apennines, Pyrenees, common. **Special Remarks:** Protected!

Date Seen:

Place:

Alpenrose

Rhododendron ferrugineum   Heather Family; ⊿

Characters: shrub, bisexual, flowers funnel-shaped, solitary flowers in umbel at end of stem, dark red, sometime paler or white; leaves evergreen, oval, margins rolle under, reddish gland scales beneath, height 50—150 cm
Flowers: May—Aug. **Habitat:** pine forests, 1500—2400 m
Distribution: Central Alps, Pyrenees, Apennines. **Specia
Remarks:** Partially protected!

Date Seen:

Place:

Hairy Alpenrose

Rhododendron hirsutum   Heather Family; ⚠

Characters: shrub, pale red, hairy, funnel-shaped flowers, inside white, terminal clusters, 5-lobed flowers; leaves leathery, shiny yellow, later brown scaly glands, margin conspicuously hairy, height 50—120 cm. **Flowers:** May—Aug. **Habitat:** screes, dwarf-shrub heath, anchors debris, 1200—2400 m. **Distribution:** calcareous Alps. **Special Remarks:** Protected!

Date Seen:

Place:

Creeping Azalea

Loiseleuria procumbens   Heather Fami

Characters: prostrate, mat-forming undershrub, 2—5 flow
ers at end of shoot, red, 5-lobed flower, conspicuously be
shaped, anthers dark red; leaves leathery, opposite, ma
gins rolled under, height 15—30 cm. **Flowers:** June—Jul
Habitat: stony places, 1500—2500 m. **Distribution:** Euro
pean mountains, Arctic, pioneer plant.

Date Seen:

Place:

Spring Heath

rica carnea   Heather Family; ⚠

Characters: dwarf undershrub, bisexual, flowers small,
bell-shaped, 4-lobed, with projecting anthers, flesh-pink;
leaves linear in whorls around stem, height 15—40 cm.
Flowers: Jan.—Apr. **Habitat:** dwarf-shrub heath, screes,
500—2200 m. **Distribution:** Alps, Apennines, on limestone. **Special Remarks:** Partially protected!

Date Seen:

Place:

Least Primrose

Primula minima   Primrose Family;

Characters: perennial rosette, bisexual, solitary flowers
red petals fused to tubes, tips of petals spread like op
saucers, petals deeply notched, white eye, 5 fused sepa
leaves pale green, apex toothed, glossy, not sticky, r
zome, height to 3 cm. **Flowers:** June–July. **Habitat:** d
grasslands, rock, 1200–3100 m. **Distribution:** Alps, Ca
pathians, Balkans, rare. **Special Remarks:** Endangere
Protected!

Date Seen: **Place:**

owbread

yclamen purpurascens   Primrose Family; ⚠

aracters: perennial, carmine pink, fragrant, solitary
wers, 5 reflexed petals, drooping, flower coiled in fruit;
aves evergreen, heart- or kidney-shaped, slightly
alloped, dark green with lighter, shiny pattern, height
-20 cm. **Flowers:** June–Sept. **Habitat:** woods, brush-
nd, 1000–1500 m. **Distribution:** calcareous Alps. **Spe-
al Remarks:** Protected!

te Seen:

ace:

Mountain Thrift

Armeria alpina   Thrift Family;

Characters: perennial rosette bush, bisexual, flowers
capitulum, bracts scarious, pink to red; basal leave
narrow, grassy, three longitudinal veins, taproot, heig
5—20 cm. **Flowers:** May—Oct. **Habitat:** screes, dry gras
lands, rock, 1100—3100 m. **Distribution:** Alps, Pyrenee
Eastern Carpathians. **Special Remarks:** Protected!

Date Seen:

Place:

Garland Flower

Daphne striata   Daphne Family; † ⚠

Characters: perennial bush, bisexual, 4 petals fused to tube, 8—12 flowers in terminal clusters, pink; leaves evergreen, wedge-shaped, crowded at shoot tips, height 5— cm. **Flowers:** May—July. **Habitat:** screes, stony grasslands, rock, 1500—2500 m. **Distribution:** absent from Central Alps, rare. **Special Remarks:** Poisonous! Protected!

Date Seen:

Place:

Crimson-Tipped Lousewort

Pedicularis oederi Figwort Family

Characters: perennial semiparasite, 5—15 pale yell
flowers in dense raceme, purple spots on upper lip, u
toothed, lower lip spreading, hairless; leaves pinnate a
finely toothed, height 5—20 cm. **Flowers:** June—July. **Ha**
tat: grasslands, dwarf-shrub heath, 1500—2500 m. **Dis**
bution: calcareous Alps. **Special Remarks:** Poisonous

Date Seen:

Place:

lesh-Pink Lousewort

edicularis rostrato spicata   Figwort Family; †

haracters: perennial, 3—15 flowers forming dense clus-
r, dark pink, flower angled at 90°, lower lip slightly
preading, upper lip with small beak; stem leaves alternate,
aves pinnate and serrated, height 20—40 cm. **Flowers:**
ıly—Aug. **Habitat:** grasslands, 1800—2300 m. **Distribu-
on:** calcareous Alps. **Special Remarks:** Poisonous!

ate Seen:

ace:

Woolly Thistle

Cirsium eriophorum   Daisy Fami

Characters: perennial, erect, bisexual, red-purple to pa
purple tubular flowers clustered to 7-cm-tall flowerhead
bracts enveloped in white cobwebby wool with prickle
stem white cottony, leaves white cottony beneath, lor
spines, pinnate, margin partly inrolled, green above, heig
60—100 cm. **Flowers:** July—Sept. **Habitat:** pastures, wa
sides, grasslands, 600—2300 m. **Distribution:** Europe.

Date Seen:

Place:

Martagon Lily

Lilium martagon   Lily Family; ⚠

Characters: monocotyledonous perennial, erect, bisexu-
, flower purple, pink, white, 6-parted, drooping petals,
ose raceme, petals recurved; leaves whorled, unnotched,
val, bulb, height 30—100 cm. **Flowers:** June—Aug. **Habi-
t:** meadows, woods, grasslands, 200—2500 m. **Distribu-
on:** Alps, Apennines, Caucasus Mountains, common.
pecial Remarks: Protected! Medicinal herb.

ate Seen:

lace:

Orange Lily

Lilium bulbiferum   Lily Family; ̷

Characters: perennial, monocotyledonous bulb plar̶
bright orange, 6 petals with black spots inside, solitary
clustered flowers; leaves narrow, spiraling, upright, heig̶
30—90 cm. **Flowers:** June—July. **Habitat:** pastures, grass̶
lands, screes, woods, 300—2000 m. **Distribution:** Centr̶
and Southern Europe. **Special Remarks:** Endangere
Protected!

Date Seen:

Place:

Black Vanilla Orchid

Nigritella nigra   Orchid Family; ⚠

Characters: monocotyledonous perennial, bisexual, flowers blackish-purple, spires; leaves lance-shaped, alternate, tuber, height 10—20 cm. **Flowers:** June—Aug. **Habitat:** pastures, grasslands, 1200—2700 m. **Distribution:** Europe, seldom. **Special Remarks:** Endangered! Protected! Medicinal herb.

Rosy Vanilla Orchid

Nigritella rosea   ⚠

Pink flower. **Special Remarks:** Protected! Endangered!
Date Seen:
Place:

Jacquin's Rush

Juncus jacquinii   Rush Fami[l]

Characters: inconspicuous solitary flowers, blackish
brown, anthers yellow, stigmas red and spiraling, flowers i[n]
capitulum, stalked; stem and leaves cylindrical, plant form[s]
dense turf, height 15—25 cm. **Flowers:** July—Oct. **Habita[t]**
moors, damp places, 1700—3000 m. **Distribution:** Centra[l]
Alps.

Date Seen:

Place:

Netted Willow

Salix reticulata   Willow Family; ⚠

Characters: creeping, strongly branched undershrub,
dioecious, long-stalked, catkins rusty-red; leaves green,
net-veined, hairy, height 3—8 cm. **Flowers:** July—Aug.
Habitat: cushion sedge grasslands, dwarf-shrub heath,
1700—2500 m. **Distribution:** Alps, Pyrenees, Jura Mountains. **Special Remarks:** Partially protected!

Date Seen:

Place:

Common Monkshood

Aconitum napellus   Buttercup Family;

Characters: perennial, erect bush, flower of violet sepals, helmet-shaped, without spurs, petals form nectary; leaves large, palmately cut, 5—7-parted, dark green above, pale green beneath, shiny, turnip-shaped root, height 50—180 cm. **Flowers:** June—Aug. **Habitat:** tall-herb communities, damp places, to 2000 m. **Distribution:** Southern and Central European mountains. **Special Remarks:** Seeks out nitrogen. Highly poisonous! Do not pick! Medicinal herb.

Date Seen: **Place:**

Small Pasque Flower

ulsatilla montana   Buttercup Family; † ⚠

haracters: perennial rosette, bisexual, 5- to many-parted
olitary flowers, dark violet; basal leaves, pinnate, rhi-
ome, height 10—25 cm. **Flowers:** Mar.—May. **Habitat:** dry
rasslands, 200—1500 m. **Distribution:** Alps, Carpathians,
alkans, rare. **Special Remarks:** Poisonous! Protected!
edicinal herb, demands care in use!

ate Seen:

lace:

Spring Pasque Flower

Pulsatilla vernalis   Buttercup Family; † ⚠

Characters: perennial, flower violet outside, white insid[e]
hairy, funnel-shaped bract with many lobes; leaves ar[e]
stem hairy, leaves leathery, 1-pinnate or 3-parted, heig[ht]
5–20 cm. **Flowers:** Apr.–July. **Habitat:** grasslands, d[ry]
grasslands, stony soils, to 3500 m. **Distribution:** Alp[s,]
Scandinavia, avoids limestone. **Special Remarks:** Poiso[n-]
ous! Protected!

Date Seen:

Place:

ticky Primrose
imula glutinosa   Primrose Family; ⚠

aracters: perennial, purple to violet, 2—7 flowers per
m, 5 petals fused to tube, lobes open saucers; leaves
h dark spots above, toothed, entire plant sticky, height
8 cm. **Flowers:** July—Aug. **Habitat:** screes, curved
dge grasslands, 1600—3000 m. **Distribution:** Eastern
s. **Special Remarks:** Protected!

te Seen:

ice:

Alpine Snowbell

Soldanella alpina   Primrose Fam

Characters: perennial rosette, bisexual, 1—3 flowe
deeply fringed, 5 throat scales, styles longer than flow
violet; leaves rounded to kidney-shaped, basal, heig
5—15 cm. **Flowers:** Apr.—June. **Habitat:** snowbeds, dar
pastures, 900—1800 m. **Distribution:** Alps, Apennine
Pyrenees.

Date Seen:

Place:

eld Gentian

ntianella campestris   Gentian Family; ⚠

aracters: annual/biennial rosette, pale violet to blue-
let, 4 oval petals, fused, throat bearded, many flowers at
se of leaves and at end of shoots; leaves opposite, oval,
nted, rosette leaves generally dead at blossom, height
20 cm. **Flowers:** June—Sept. **Habitat:** grasslands,
0—3100 m. **Distribution:** Southern to Central Europe.
ecial Remarks: Protected! Endangered! Medicinal herb.

te Seen:

ce:

Alpine Toadflax

Linaria alpina   Figwort Fam

Characters: perennial, bluish- to reddish-violet alwa
with orange patch, 2—8 flowers in small raceme, long sp
leaves unnotched, whorled, lance-shaped, rooting ste
height 5—10 cm. **Flowers:** June—July. **Habitat:** screes, a
chors debris, 1500—3000 m. **Distribution:** calcare
Alps.

Date Seen:

Place:

ound-Headed Rampion

yteuma orbiculare   Bellflower Family

aracters: biennial, flowers pale blue-violet, with strap-
aped lobes joined at base, many solitary flowers in termi-
head, style protrudes from flower; stalked, oval-oblong
sal leaves, height 10—40 cm. **Flowers:** May—Sept.
bitat: grasslands, open woods, 0—2000 m. **Distribu-
n:** calcareous Alps.

te Seen:

ce:

Alpine Aster

Aster alpinus   Daisy Fam

Characters: perennial rosette, bisexual, composite hea
violet rays, disc of yellow tubular florets; leaves alterna
narrow, rhizome, height 5—20 cm. **Flowers:** Ju
Aug. **Habitat:** pastures, grasslands, screes, rock, 140
3000 m. **Distribution:** Alps, Apennines, Carpathians, co
mon.

Date Seen:

Place:

assel Hyacinth

uscari comosum   Lily Family; ⚠

aracters: perennial, monocotyledonous, bulb, blue-violet, g-stemmed bells in raceme; basal leaves in rosette, ce-shaped, height 20—70 cm. **Flowers:** Apr.—June. **bitat:** meadows, dry grasslands, rocky soil, to 1500 m. **stribution:** Southern, Western Europe. **Special Re-rks:** Protected! Endangered! Medicinal herb.

te Seen:

ce:

Alpine Clematis

Clematis alpina Buttercup Family;

Characters: perennial climber, bisexual, flowers solita
nodding at base of leaf, petals form white nectary, 4—5 s
pals (blue) form flower; leaves alternate, 1-2-pinnate, ha
beneath, tendril-like leaf stems, height 2—4 m. **Flowe**
May—July. **Habitat:** mountain forests, brushwood, rare,
limestone, 1000—1400 m. **Distribution:** Alps, Pyrene
Apennines. **Special Remarks:** Protected!

Date Seen:

Place:

lpine Eryngo

yngium alpinum Carrot Family; ⚠

aracters: perennial, bisexual, umbel-like cluster of 2—4 indrical heads, flowers small, blue, spiny bracts; 3-part- stem leaves, basal leaves undivided, all leaves spiny, nip-like root, height 30—60 cm. **Flowers:** July—Sept. **bitat:** grasslands, pastures, 1500—2500 m. **Distribu- n:** Southern and Western Alps. **Special Remarks:** Rare, ictly protected! Endangered!

te Seen:

ce:

Clusius's Gentian

Gentiana clusii   Gentian Family;

Characters: perennial rosette, bisexual, flowers solita
trumpets, 5—6 cm, azure blue, inside no green spots,
most no stem, sepal teeth triangular, no white membra
leaves oval to oblong, rhizome, height 8 cm. **Flowe**
May—Aug. **Habitat:** rare, often on soil rich in lime, in cus
ion sedge grasslands, blue-grass, 1200—2800 m. **Dis**
bution: Alps, Apennines, Carpathians. **Special Remar**
Protected!

Date Seen: **Place:**

Trumpet Gentian

Gentiana acaulis　　　　　　Gentian Family; ⚠

Characters: perennial, bisexual, rosette, dark blue, large erect flowers, inside always with green stripe; basal leaves rosette, broad, height 5–10 cm. **Flowers:** May–Aug. **Habitat:** grasslands, meadows, 800–3100 m. **Distribution:** Alps, Apennines. **Special Remarks:** Endangered! Protected! Old medicinal herb.

Date Seen:

Place:

Spring Gentian

Gentiana verna   Gentian Family;

Characters: perennial rosette, bisexual, bright blue solitary flowers, tight petal tube with lobes in open saucer, sep lobed tube; on upright stem 1—3 pairs of smaller, opposi leaves, basal leaves elliptical to lance-shaped, rhizom height 5—10 cm. **Flowers:** Apr.—Aug. **Habitat:** mounta meadows, semi-dry grasslands, 300—2700 m. **Distribu tion:** Alps, Apennines, Pyrenees, common. **Special R marks:** Completely protected!

Date Seen: **Place:**

illow-Leaved Gentian

entiana asclepiadea   Gentian Family; ⚠

aracters: perennial, erect plant, bisexual, bell-shaped
wers, with short stems from base of upper leaves,
obed, bright blue, inside pale stripes or spots; leaves
al, lance-shaped, decussate (in alternate pairs), rhi-
me, height 30—70 cm. **Flowers:** July—Sept. **Habitat:**
mp mountain meadows and grasslands. **Distribution:**
careous Alps. **Special Remarks:** Completely protected!

te Seen:

ace:

Alpine Bartsia

Bartsia alpina   Figwort Fam

Characters: perennial semiparasite, blue, flowers ste
less, joined at base of leaf, conspicuously 2-lipped, upp
lip arched, lower lip 3-lobed; leaves decussate (in alterna
pairs), notched, oval, plant sometimes blue-tinged, heig
5—20 cm. **Flowers:** June—Aug. **Habitat:** springs, sno
beds, swampy places, 1000—3000 m. **Distribution:** Alp

Date Seen:

Place:

Bearded Bellflower

Campanula barbata   Bellflower Family

Characters: perennial rosette, bisexual, blue or white, bell-shaped, 5-lobed hairy flowers in loose raceme; leaves basal, narrow, height 10—30 cm. **Flowers:** June—Aug. **Habitat:** meadows, grasslands, woods, 1000—3000 m. **Distribution:** Alps, Southern, Central Europe.

Date Seen:

Place:

Scheuchzer's Bellflower

Campanula scheuchzeri   Bellflower Fami[ly]

Characters: perennial, dark blue, bells somewha[t] crowded, 5-lobed, terminal or in terminal racemes; ste[m] hairless, stem leaves lance-shaped, hairy-edged at bas[e] basal leaves rounded to heart-shaped, height 3–15 cm
Flowers: June–Sept. **Habitat:** stony places, grasslands dwarf-shrub heath, screes, to over 3000 m. **Distributio[n]** Alps, Pyrenees.

Date Seen:

Place:

iry's Thimble

mpanula cochlearifolia   Bellflower Family

aracters: perennial, rosette, creeper, bisexual, nod-
g, racemes of blue-violet flowers, outside dark-veined;
ves alternate, lance-shaped, rhizome, height 5—15 cm.
wers: June—Aug. **Habitat:** screes, rock, 1300—3500 m.
tribution: Alps, Apennines, Balkans, common.

te Seen:

ce:

Matted Globularia

Globularia cordifolia   Bellflower Fam

Characters: perennial, creeping dwarf subshrub, bise
al, 7 mm long, head of bell-shaped flowers, upper
2-lobed, lower lip 3-lobed, pale blue to white; basal leav
oblong, never round at tip, rhizome, height 3–15 cm. **Fl
ers:** May–Aug. **Habitat:** dry grasslands, screes, ro
1800–2500 m, on limestone, likes warmth. **Distributi
Alps, Apennines, Balkans.

Date Seen:

Place:

...piniest Thistle

...sium spinosissimum   Daisy Family

...racters: perennial, bisexual, flowerhead only disc flo-
..., no rays, pale green, long pointed bracts; leaves alter-
... along entire stalk, spine-toothed, feathery, cylindrical
..., height to 120 cm. **Flowers:** July—Sept. **Habitat:** damp
...tures, screes, cirques, 1600—3000 m. **Distribution:**
.... **Special Remarks:** Seeks out nitrogen.

...e Seen:

...ce:

Index
of English Names:

Index
of Scientific Names: